Power Maths

Year I
Practice Book

IA

White Rose Ma

What do you look like?
Draw a picture of you.

This book belongs to _____ .

My class is _____ .

Series editor: Tony Staneff

Lead author: Josh Lury

Consultant (first edition): Professor Liu Jian and Professor Zhang Dan

Author team (first edition): Tony Staneff, Josh Lury, Beth Smith,
Liu Jian, Zhang Dan and Huang Lihua

Pearson

Contents

We will practise different ways to solve problems!

We can show what we have done in **My Power Points**.

3

How to use this book

Let's see how this Practice Book works!

This shows you pages from the Textbook. You will learn how to answer the questions in your class.

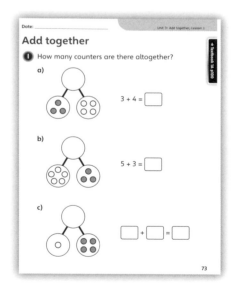

Have a go at questions by yourself using this Practice Book.

Challenge questions make you think hard!

Questions with this light bulb make you think differently.

Reflect

Answer a **Reflect** question to show how much you have learnt.

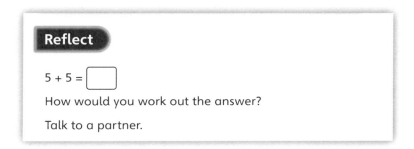

Fill in **My Journal** at the end of a unit.

This will help you show how much you can do now.

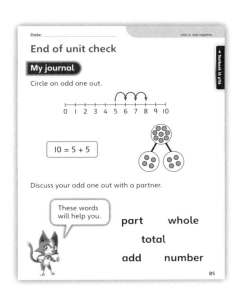

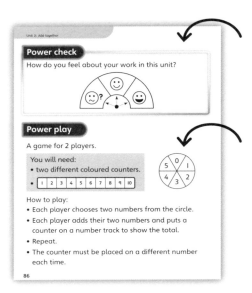

Show here how you got on with your practice.

Have fun trying the **Power Play**.

Date: _____

Sort objects

1 Sort into two groups. Draw around each group.

a)

c)

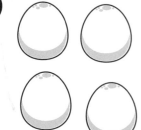 

b)

2 Draw around the groups.

6

3 Draw around the groups.

a)

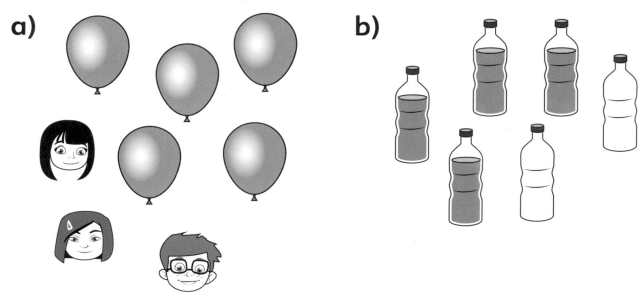

b)

4 Cross out the object that does not belong.

a)

c)

b)

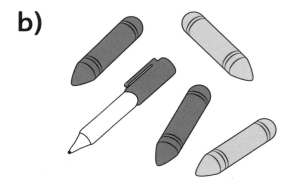

d)

5 Sort the objects.

CHALLENGE

Is there another way?

Tell a partner how you sorted them.

Reflect

Draw two groups of objects.

Date: _____

Count objects to 10

1 How many of each are there?

a)

b)

c)

2 How many of each are there?

a)

b)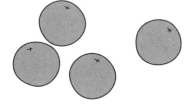

c)

3 How many of each are there?

a) _____ footballs

b) _____ flowers

c) _____ pencils

Point and count.

4 How many pegs are there? ⬚

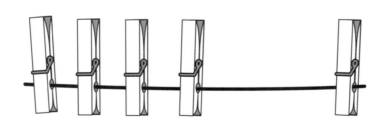

a) How many ? ☐

b) How many ? ☐

CHALLENGE

6 How many beads? ☐

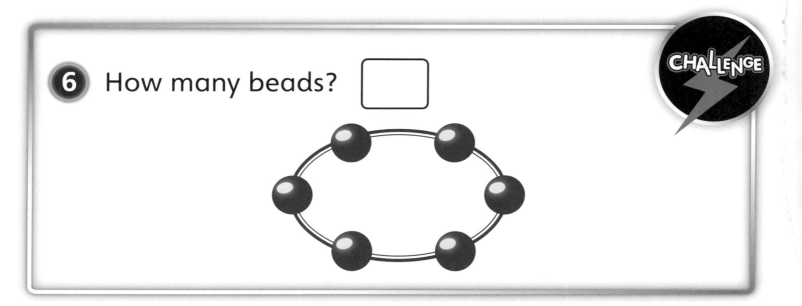

Reflect

Fill in the missing numbers.

1	2	3	4						

Date: _____

Represent numbers to 10

 Write the numbers.

a)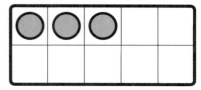

c)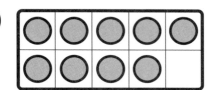

b)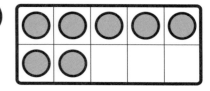

d)

2 Count the objects.

Colour the counters on the ten frames to show the number.

a)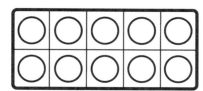

b)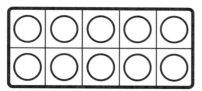

3 Show these numbers on a ten frame.

a) 6

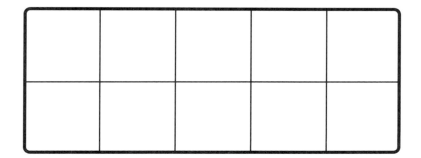

b) 10

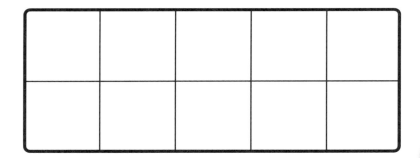

c) 2

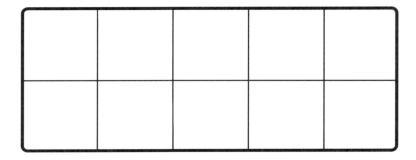

I like using counters.

4 Show 4 in different ways.

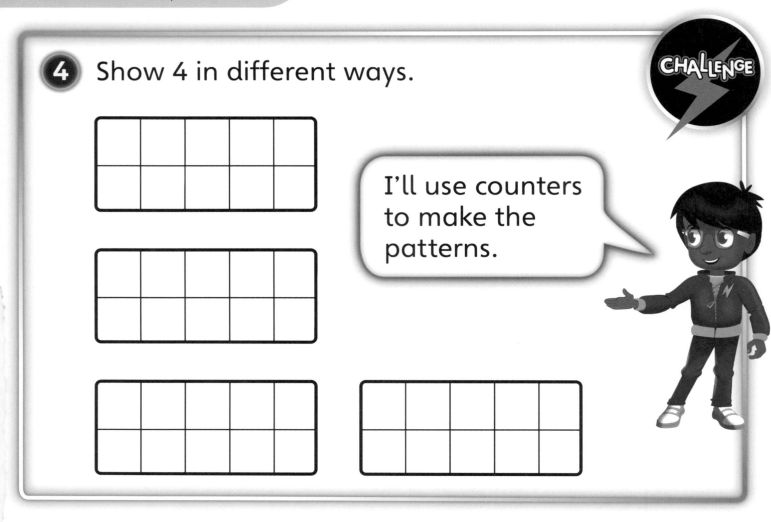

CHALLENGE

I'll use counters to make the patterns.

Reflect

Pick a number. Show it.

My number is ☐ .

Count objects from a larger group

1 **a)** Tick 4 cats.

b) Tick 6 balls.

c) Tick 8 mice.

2 **a)** Colour 3 trees.

b) Colour 7 umbrellas.

c) Colour 2 apples.

3 **a)** Colour 5 apples.

b) Colour 5 apples.

c) Colour 5 apples.

4 **a)** Circle 3 trees.

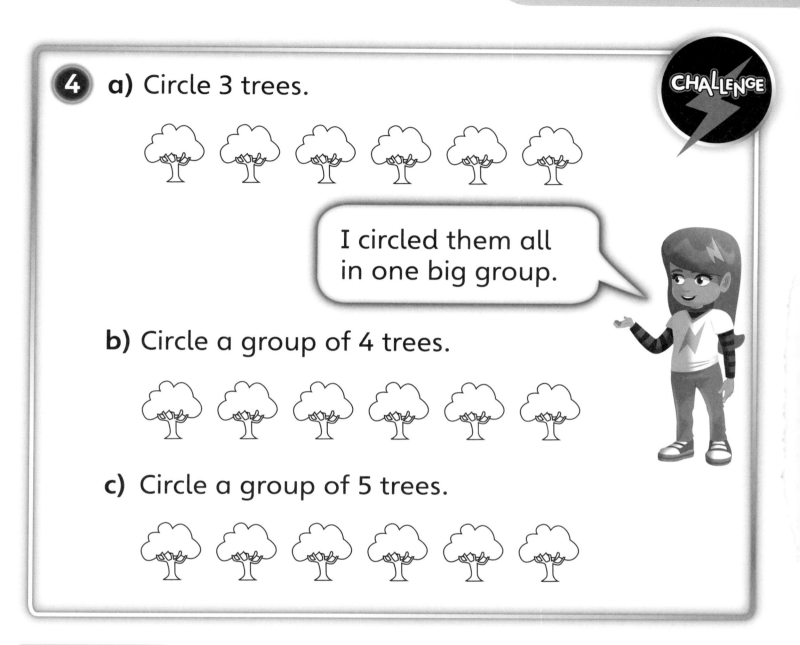

CHALLENGE

I circled them all in one big group.

b) Circle a group of 4 trees.

c) Circle a group of 5 trees.

Reflect

Use 10 cubes.

Ask a partner to say a number between 1 and 10.

Count that number of cubes.

Date: _____

Count on from any number

1 Count on from each number.

a)

b)

c)

2 Fill in the number track.

5					

Start with the number 5 and count on.

→ Textbook 1A p24

3 Complete the numbers in order.

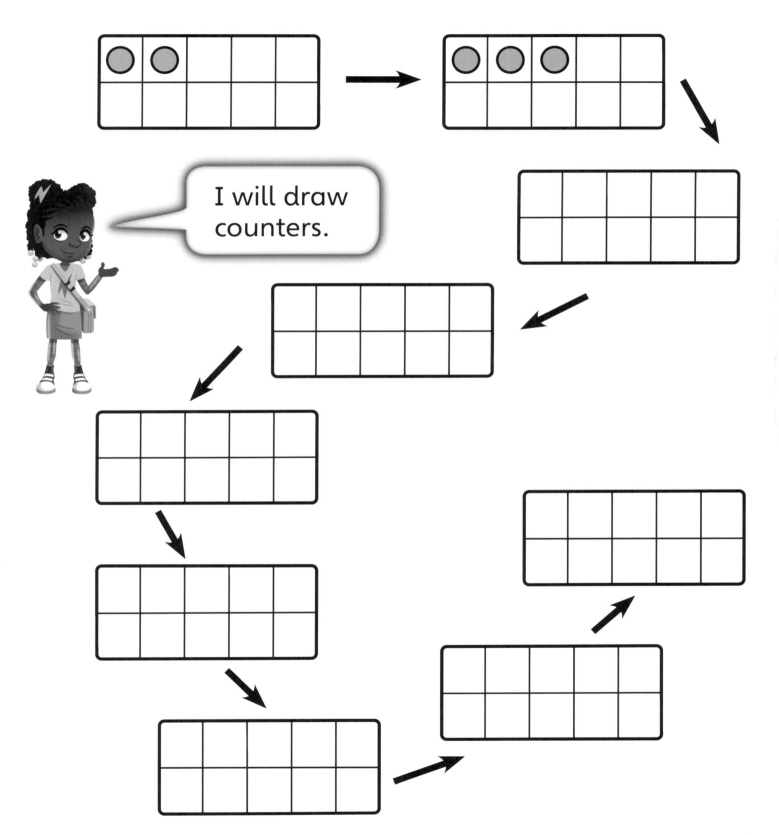

I will draw counters.

④ Fill in the numbers.

CHALLENGE

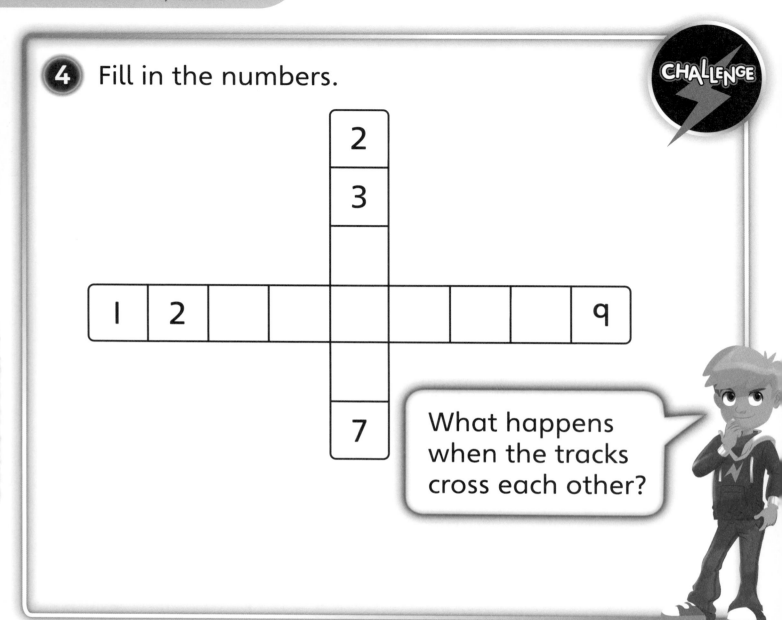

| 2 |
| 3 |

| 1 | 2 | | | | | | | | q |

What happens when the tracks cross each other?

| 7 |

Reflect

Choose a starting number.

Count up to 10.

Practise with a partner.

One more

1 Draw one more. Write the number.

a)

b)

c)

d)

2 Fill in the missing numbers.

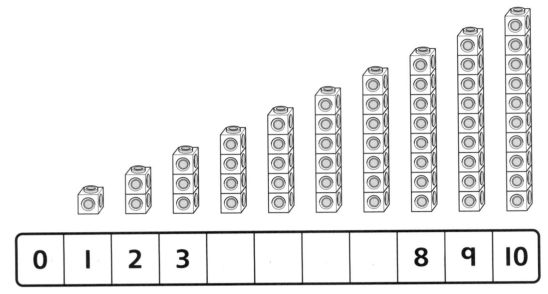

| 0 | 1 | 2 | 3 | | | | | 8 | 9 | 10 |

3 Write one more.

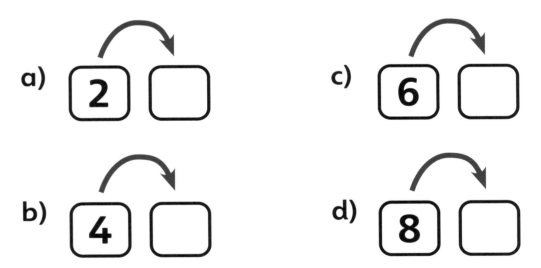

a) 2 [ ]

b) 4 [ ]

c) 6 [ ]

d) 8 [ ]

4 Write the missing numbers.

a) 3 ☐

b) q ☐

c) ☐ 3

d) ☐ q

CHALLENGE

I can use my fingers to find numbers.

Reflect

Play this game with a partner. Take turns.
Use different numbers of pencils.

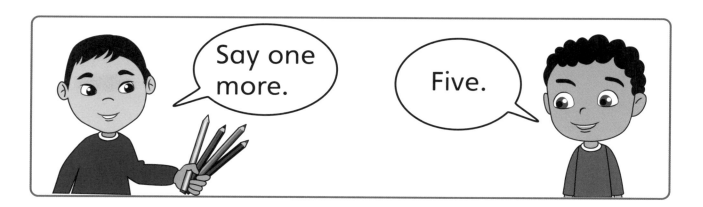

Say one more.

Five.

Date: _____

Count backwards from 10 to 0

1 Fill in the number tracks.

a)

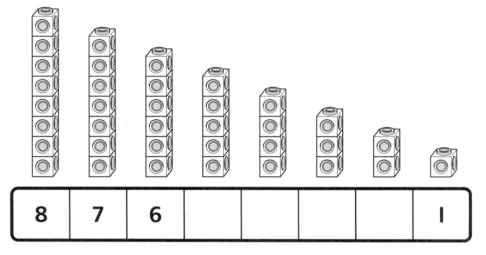

8	7	6					1

b)

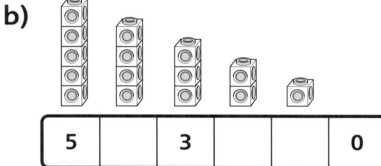

5		3			0

2 Fill in the number tracks.

a)
7	6		4	3			

b)
10		8		6	

c)
5				1

24

3 Tas counts from 6 to 0.

Complete what she says.

4 Fill in the missing numbers.

a)
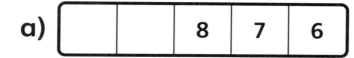

		8	7	6

b)
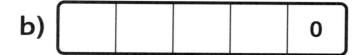

				0

c)

d)

		3	4

I can see that some of these numbers go up.

25

5 Fill in the missing numbers.

7
5

1		3		5		7	

3

Reflect

Roll a .

What number did you roll? [ ]

- Count on to 10 from the number.

- Count back to 0 from the number.

Date: _____

Unit 1: Numbers to 10, Lesson 8

One less

1 Write one less.

a)

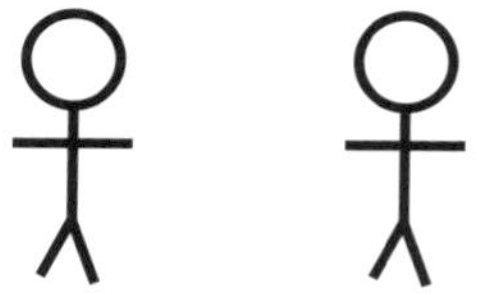

[ ] [2]

b)

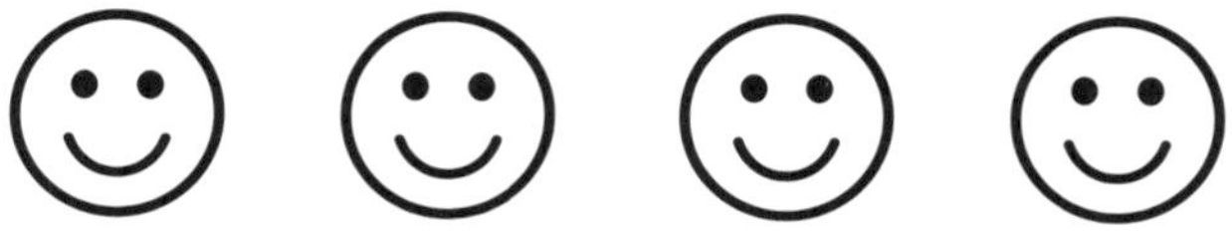

[1] [2] [ ] [4]

c)

[1] [2] [3] [ ] [5]

d)

[1] [2] [3] [4] [5] [6] [7] [ ] [9]

→ Textbook 1A p36

27

2 Write in the missing numbers.

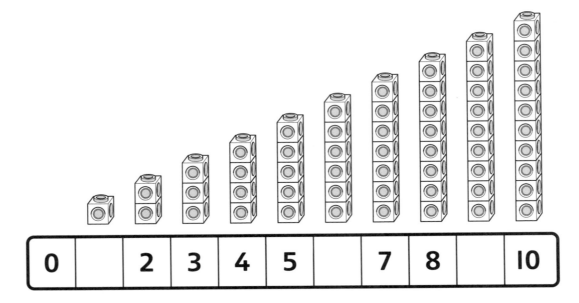

| 0 | | 2 | 3 | 4 | 5 | | 7 | 8 | | 10 |

3 Write one less.

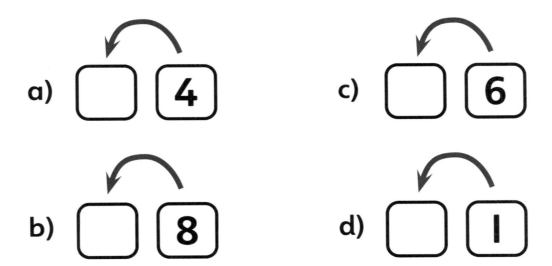

a) ⬜ 4

c) ⬜ 6

b) ⬜ 8

d) ⬜ 1

4 Write the missing numbers.

CHALLENGE

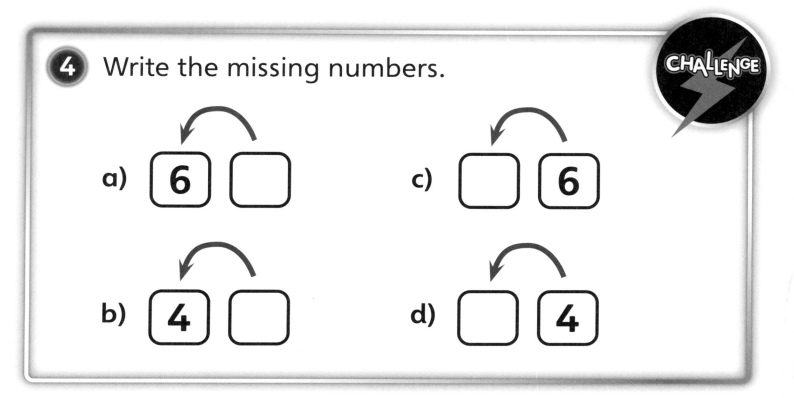

a) 6 ☐

c) ☐ 6

b) 4 ☐

d) ☐ 4

Reflect

Play this game with a partner. Take turns.
Use different numbers of pencils.

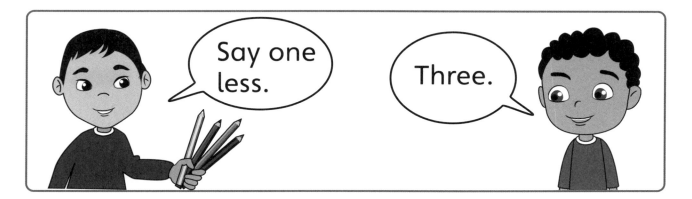

Say one less.

Three.

29

Date: _____

Compare groups

→ Textbook 1A p40

1 Draw a line from each child to a present.

Can each child have a present?

Circle your answer: Yes   No

2 Draw a line from each mouse to a piece of cheese.

Can each mouse have a piece of cheese?

Circle your answer: Yes   No

3 Draw one worm for each bird.

4 Can each dish have a mug?

Circle your answer: Yes   No

Could you draw lines?

5 Draw a line from each child to a cake.

a) Can each child have a cake?   Yes   No

b) Are there the same number of
children and cakes?   Yes   No

Reflect

Take some counters and some pencils.
Put I counter with I pencil.

Keep doing this until all the counters or pencils
have been used.

Do you have pencils or counters left? How many?

Fewer or more?

1 Are there more hens or sheep?

Tick the correct box.

2 Are there more apples or bananas?

Tick the correct box.

3 Are there fewer cakes or fewer children?

Tick the correct boxes.

4 Are there fewer mice or pieces of cheese?

CHALLENGE

5 Are there more ⭐ or 🔺 ?

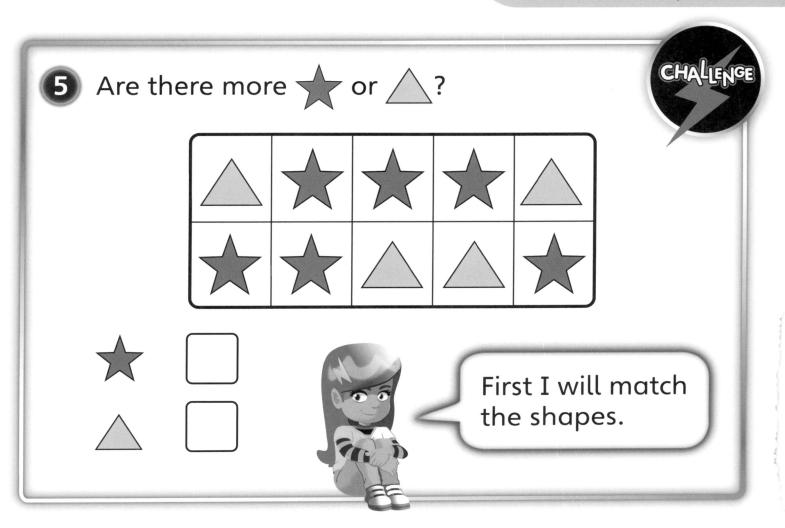

First I will match the shapes.

Reflect

Anya has 5 sweets.

Tim has fewer sweets.

Draw Tim's sweets.

Is there more than one way to draw this?

35

Date: _____

<, > or =

1 Complete the number sentences.

a)

 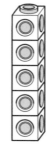

b)

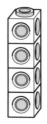

c)

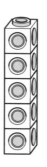 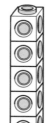

2 Complete the number sentences.

a)

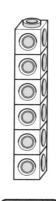 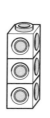

b)

 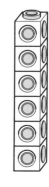

3 Draw towers to show the number sentences are true.

a) $4 > 3$

b) $4 = 4$

CHALLENGE

4 **a)** Complete the number sentence.

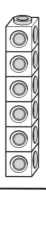 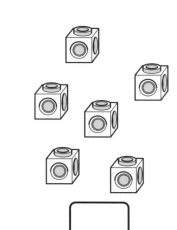

b) Which symbol would you use here?

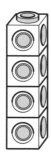 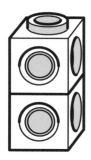

Reflect

Make or draw your own towers to show
how to use <, > and =.

→ Textbook 1A p52

Compare numbers

1 Circle the larger number in each.

a)

c)

b)

d)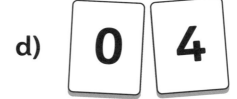

2 Circle the smaller number in each.

a)

c)

b)

d)

3 Complete the number sentences.

Use <, > or = and the correct digits.

a)

6 ◯ 8

c)

b)

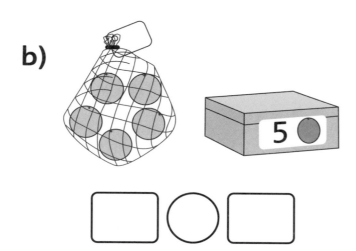

4 Complete the number sentences. Use <, > or =.

a) 7 ◯ 7

b) 0 ◯ 4

c) 6 ◯ 5

d) 10 ◯ 2

5 Complete these number sentences.

a) ☐ < 6

b) 10 > ☐

c) 5 < ☐

I wonder if there is more than one answer for each.

Reflect

One person says a number.

The next person says a larger number.

The next person says a smaller number.

And so on.

Can the whole class do it?

Date: _____

Order objects and numbers

1 Circle the smallest number.

a)

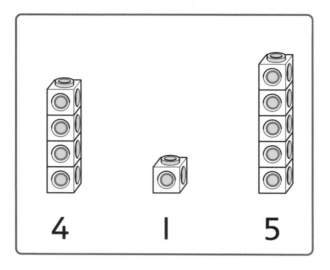

4   1   5

c)

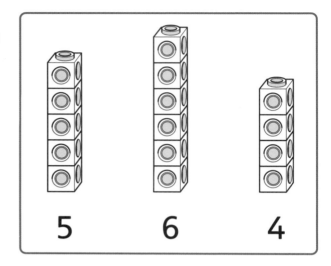

5   6   4

b)

4   3   1

d)

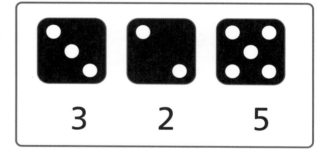

3   2   5

2 Circle the smallest number.

a)   8   10   2

c)   6   5   7

b)   9   8   7

d)   2   9   8

3 Circle the greatest number.

a)

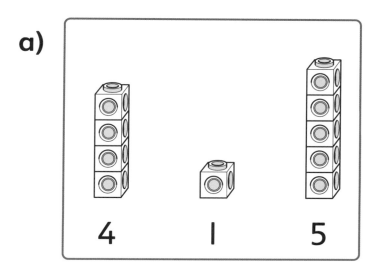

4   1   5

c)

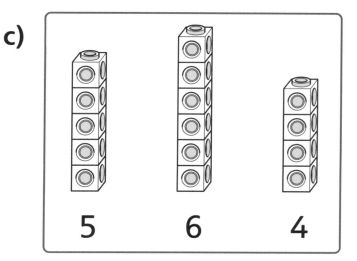

5   6   4

b)

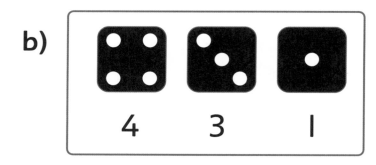

4   3   1

d)

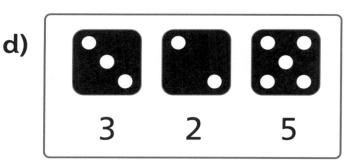

3   2   5

4 Circle the greatest number.

a)

| 10 | 3 | 2 |

c)

| 2 | 9 | 3 |

b)

| 5 | 4 | 3 |

d)

| 2 | 7 | 6 |

5 Write the numbers in order.

a)

b)

c) 2, 8, 4

d) 10, 1, 5, 9

Reflect

What can the missing numbers be?

a)   6, ☐ , 8

b)   7, 8, ☐ , 10

Date: _____

The number line

1 Complete the number lines.

a)

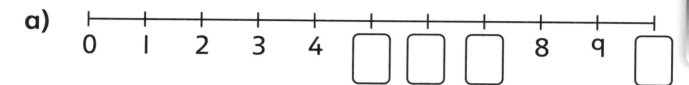

0   1   2   3   4   ☐ ☐ ☐   8   9   ☐

b)

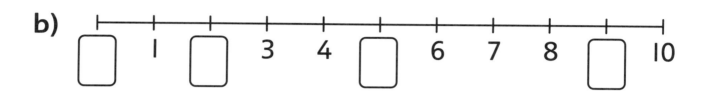

☐   1   ☐   3   4   ☐   6   7   8   ☐   10

c)

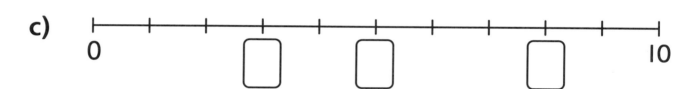

0   ☐   ☐   ☐   10

2 a) Draw an arrow to the number 2.

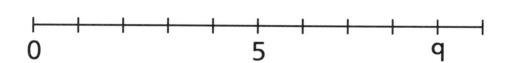

0   5   9

b) Draw an arrow to the number 6.

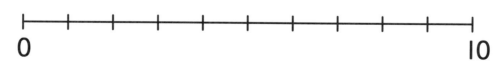

0   10

I could fill in the number lines.

45

3 Use the number lines to work out the answers.

a) Which is greater, 3 or 7?

```
0   1   2   3   4   5   6   7   8   9   10
```

b) Which is smaller, 5 or 2?

```
0   1   2   3   4   5   6   7   8   9   10
```

4 a) What is one more than 5?

```
0   1   2   3   4   5   6   7   8   9   10
```

b) What is one less than 10?

```
0   1   2   3   4   5   6   7   8   9   10
```

I will draw the jumps.

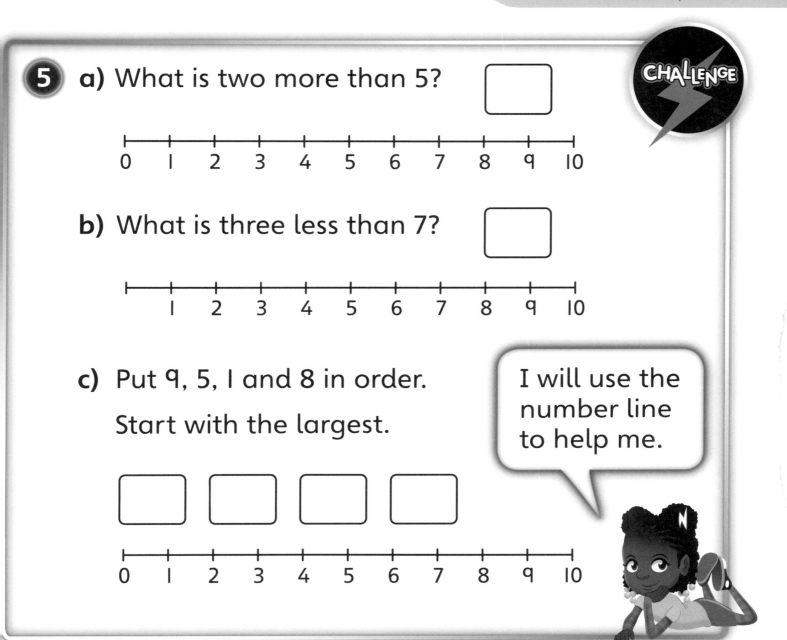

5 **a)** What is two more than 5?

0 1 2 3 4 5 6 7 8 9 10

b) What is three less than 7?

1 2 3 4 5 6 7 8 9 10

c) Put 9, 5, 1 and 8 in order.

Start with the largest.

0 1 2 3 4 5 6 7 8 9 10

CHALLENGE

I will use the number line to help me.

Reflect

Tell a partner what you have learnt today.

Date: _____

End of unit check

My journal

Bea has 5 spotted balloons and I plain balloon.

Colour them in.

Seth has 3 spotted balloons and 3 plain balloons.

Colour them in.

- What is the same? _____
  _____
- What is different? _____
  _____

These words will help you.

balloon	I	one
less	3	three
more	5	five

48

Power check

How do you feel about your work in this unit?

Power play

A game for 2 or more players.

You will need:	• digit cards 0 to 9 • a blank ten frame • counters

How to play:

- Mix up the cards and put them face down on the table.

- Each player chooses a card.

- Make the number shown, using the counters and the ten frame.

- The winner is the player with the largest number.

Date: _____

Parts and wholes

1 Write how many there are in each part.

a)

b)

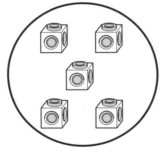
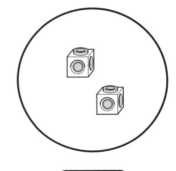

c)

2 Complete the sentences.

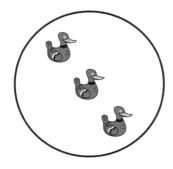 

is a part.

is a part.

The whole is .

3 Complete the sentences.

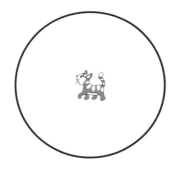 

is a part.

is a part.

The whole is .

4 Point to the parts.

Tell a partner what you think the whole is.

5 Make a tower of 6 cubes.

Break it into two parts.

Say out loud:

'_____ is a part.

_____ is a part.

The whole is _____.'

Reflect

Draw or make two parts. How many are in the whole?

Date: _____

The part-whole model

1 Complete the part-whole models.

a)

 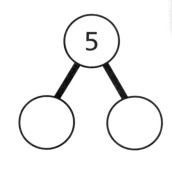

b)

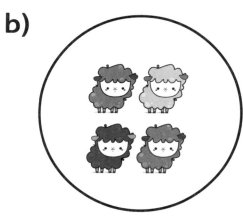  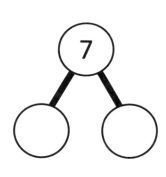

2 Draw 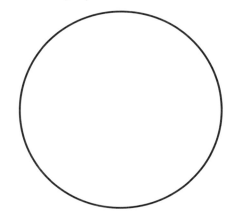 to show the two parts.

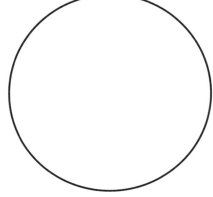 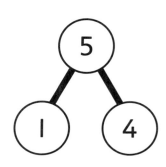

3 Complete the part-whole models.

a)

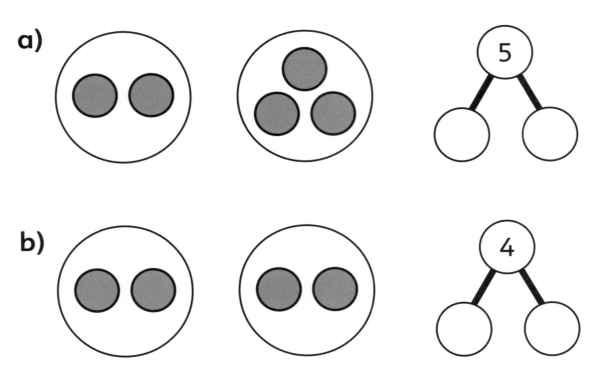

b)

4 Complete the part-whole models.

Use 7 counters to help you.

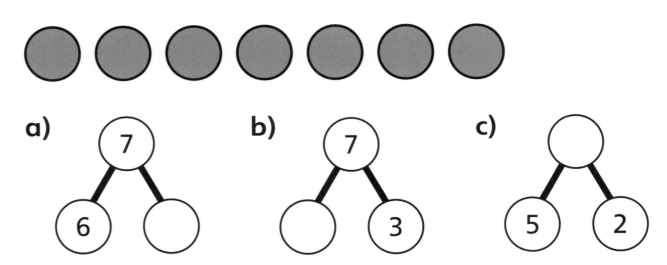

a) 7 / 6, __

b) 7 / __, 3

c) __ / 5, 2

5 Complete each part-whole model in a different way.

CHALLENGE

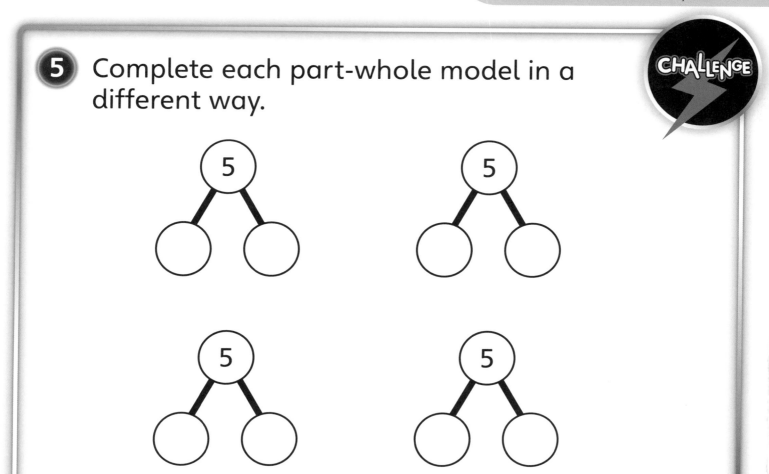

Reflect

In a part-whole model, the whole is always the largest number.

True or false?

Date: _____

Write number sentences

1 Complete the part-whole models and number sentences.

a)

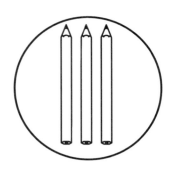 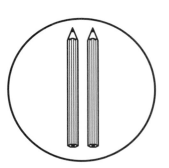 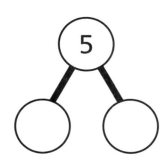

☐ + ☐ = 5

b)

  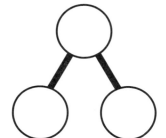

☐ + ☐ = ☐

2 Write a number sentence to match the part-whole model.

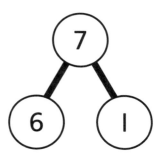

☐ + ☐ = ☐

56

3 Complete the number sentences.

a)

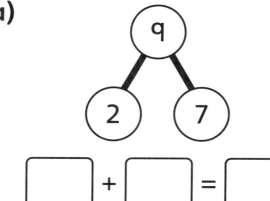

$\boxed{} + \boxed{} = \boxed{}$

b)

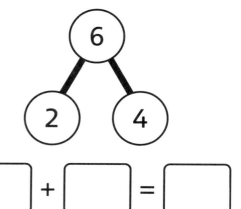

$\boxed{} + \boxed{} = \boxed{}$

4 Make 5 in different ways.

One has been done for you.

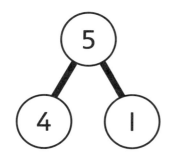

$\boxed{4} + \boxed{1} = 5$

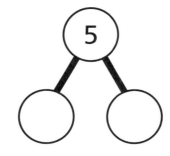

$\boxed{} + \boxed{} = 5$

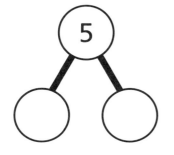

$\boxed{} + \boxed{} = 5$

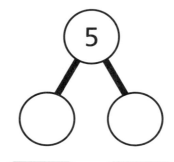

$\boxed{} + \boxed{} = 5$

5 Take 6 counters.

Make two groups from the counters.

CHALLENGE

⬤ ⬤ ⬤ ⬤ ⬤ ⬤

Write a number sentence to show the groups that you have made.

_____

_____

Reflect

Write your own number sentence.

Talk about it with a partner.

Fact families – addition facts

1 Complete the part-whole model and number sentences.

  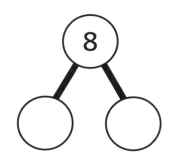

☐ + ☐ = 8   8 = ☐ + ☐

☐ + ☐ = 8   8 = ☐ + ☐

2 Complete the part-whole model.

 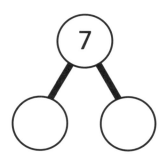

Now complete the number sentences.

☐ + ☐ = 7   7 = ☐ + ☐

☐ + ☐ = 7   7 = ☐ + ☐

3 Complete the number sentences.

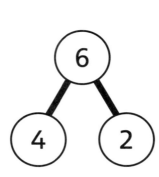

☐ + ☐ = ☐

☐ = ☐ + ☐

☐ + ☐ = ☐

☐ = ☐ + ☐

4 Complete the part-whole model.

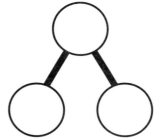

Write the number sentences.

_____

_____

_____

_____

I wonder how many different number sentences I can write.

5 Complete the number sentences.
One has been done for you.

CHALLENGE

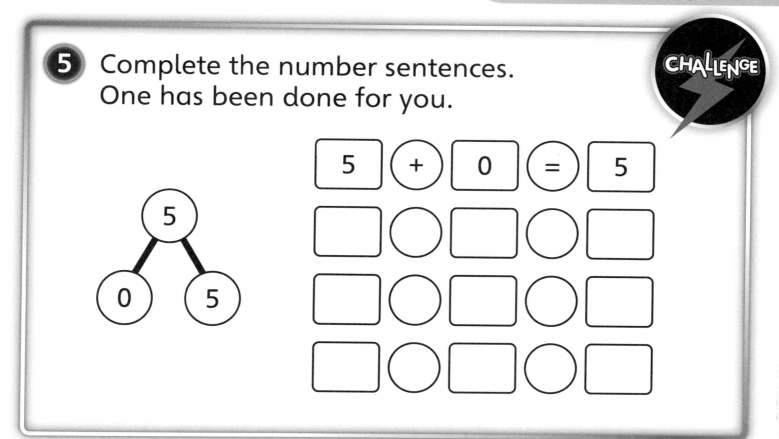

$$5 + 0 = 5$$

Reflect

Draw your own part-whole model.

Ask a partner to write the number sentences to match.

Date: _____

Number bonds

1 Complete the number bonds to 5.

Use the pictures to help.

a)

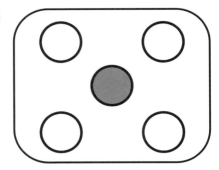

$4 + \boxed{} = 5$

b)

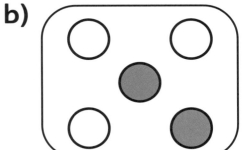

$3 + \boxed{} = 5$

2 Complete the number bonds to 6.

a)

$4 + \boxed{} = 6$

b)

$3 + \boxed{} = 6$

3 Write down the number bonds you can see.

a)

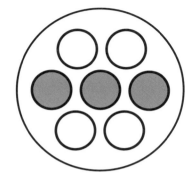

□ + □ = □

c)

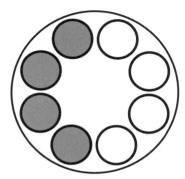

□ + □ = □

b)

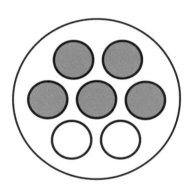

□ + □ = □

d)

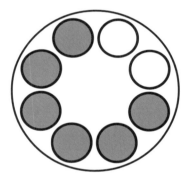

□ + □ = □

4 Find and write three different number bonds to 4.

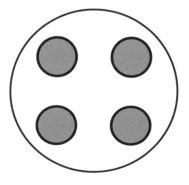

_____

_____

_____

5 Complete these number bonds to 9.

Shade in the squares to help you.

CHALLENGE

a) $3 + \boxed{} = 9$

b) $7 + \boxed{} = 9$

c) $\boxed{} + 5 = 9$

Reflect

Make a tower of 6 cubes. Break it into 2 smaller towers.

What number bond can you see?

Find number bonds

1 Complete the number bonds to 4.

a)  $1 + \boxed{} = 4$

b) $2 + \boxed{} = 4$

c) $\boxed{} + \boxed{} = 4$

2 Complete the number bonds to 7.

a) 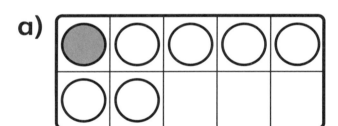 $1 + 6 = \boxed{}$

b) 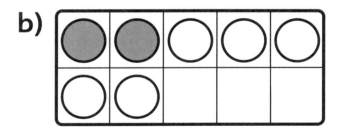 $\boxed{} + \boxed{} = \boxed{}$

c) 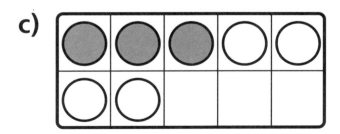  $\boxed{} + \boxed{} = \boxed{}$

Textbook 1A p88

3 Draw beads to match the number bonds to 6.

a) 4 + 2 = 6

b) 5 + 1 = 6

c) 3 + 3 = 6

4 Complete the number bonds to 9.

a) ☐ + 1 = 9

b) ☐ + 2 = 9

c) ☐ + 3 = 9

d) 4 + ☐ = 9

e) 6 + ☐ = 9

f) ☐ + 0 = 9

5 Write all the different number bonds to 8.

Use counters to help you.

CHALLENGE

_____

_____

_____

_____

_____

_____

Reflect

Draw 4 beads on each bead string to show the different ways of making 4.

_____   _____

_____   _____

Date: _____

Number bonds to 10

1 How many more do you need to make 10?

a)

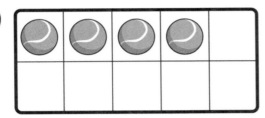

$$4 + \boxed{} = 10$$

d)

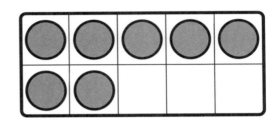

$$7 + \boxed{} = 10$$

b)

$$6 + \boxed{} = 10$$

e)

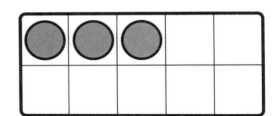

$$3 + \boxed{} = 10$$

c)

$$9 + \boxed{} = 10$$

f)

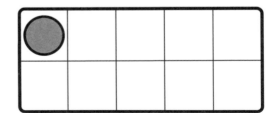

$$10 = 1 + \boxed{}$$

2 Write the missing part.

a) [ ] + 3 = 10

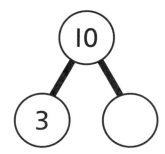

c) [ ] + 6 = 10

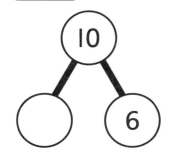

b) 5 + [ ] = 10

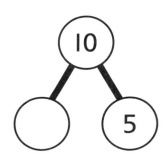

d) 9 + [ ] = 10

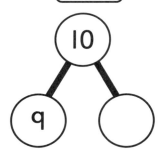

I will use a ten frame to help me.

3 Complete the part-whole model.

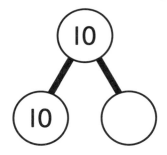

Join the numbers that add to make 10.

 CHALLENGE

1 2 3 4 5

6 7 8 9 10

Reflect

I will use my fingers.

How many number bonds to 10 can you find?

☐ + ☐ = 10

End of unit check

My journal

→ Textbook 1A p96

Use nine of these numbers in the part-whole models.

1   2   3   4   5   6   7   8   9   10

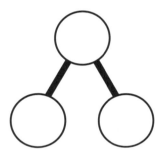   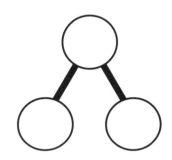   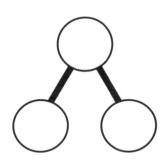

Now find a different way to complete them.

These words
will help you.

part

whole

is equal to

Power check

How do you feel about your work in this unit?

Power play

A game for 2 players.

You will need:
- counters
- part-whole model

How to play:
- Choose a number between 5 and 10.
- Put that number of counters on the whole of a part-whole model.
- Take it in turns to place 1 or 2 counters in one of the parts.
- If you make the whole, you win a point.
- If you don't make the whole, the next player goes.
- The first to 5 points is the winner.

Add together

1 How many counters are there altogether?

a)

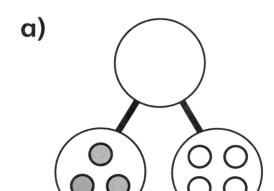

$3 + 4 = \boxed{}$

b)

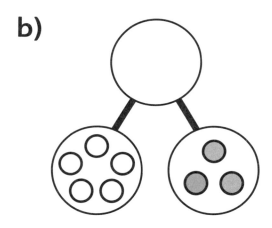

$5 + 3 = \boxed{}$

c)

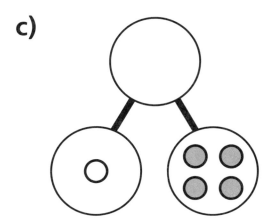

$\boxed{} + \boxed{} = \boxed{}$

2 How many apples are there altogether?

a)

$\boxed{} + \boxed{} = \boxed{}$

b)

$\boxed{} + \boxed{} = \boxed{}$

c)

$\boxed{} + \boxed{} = \boxed{}$

3 How many cars are there altogether?

$\boxed{} + \boxed{} = \boxed{}$

74

4 Work out

CHALLENGE

a) 1 + 3 = ☐

b) 2 + 5 = ☐

c) 3 + 6 = ☐

I used some counters to help me.

d) 4 + 3 = ☐

e) 1 + 6 = ☐

f) 5 + 4 = ☐

g) 6 + 2 = ☐

Reflect

5 + 5 = ☐

How would you work out the answer?

Talk to a partner.

Date: _____

Add more

1 How many altogether?

a)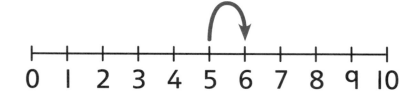

$5 + 1 = \boxed{}$

b)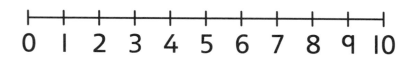

$4 + 2 = \boxed{}$

c)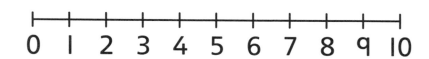

$\boxed{} + \boxed{} = \boxed{}$

2 Work out

a) 6 + 3 = ☐

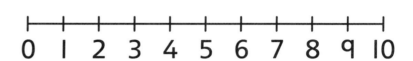

b) 7 + 1 = ☐

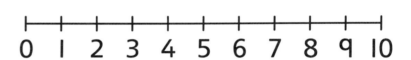

c) 5 + 3 = ☐

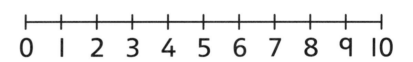

d) 2 + 4 = ☐

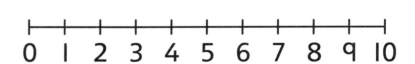

e) 1 + 8 = ☐

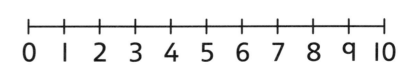

f) 4 + 5 = ☐

0 1 2 3 4 5 6 7 8 9 10

3 Match each addition to its answer.

2 + 3	9
1 + 0	5
5 + 4	10
4 + 6	6
3 + 3	1

Use the number line to help you.

0 1 2 3 4 5 6 7 8 9 10

Reflect

Tell a partner how to work out 8 + 2.

Addition problems

1 How many altogether?

a)  $8 + 2 = \boxed{}$

b)  $4 + 3 = \boxed{}$

c) $1 + 5 = \boxed{}$

2 What are the total scores?

a)

$\boxed{} + \boxed{} = \boxed{}$

b)

$\boxed{} + \boxed{} = \boxed{}$

3 Look at the darts. What are the total scores?

a)

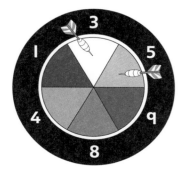

⬜ + ⬜ = ⬜

c)

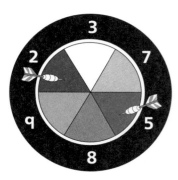

⬜ + ⬜ = ⬜

b)

⬜ + ⬜ = ⬜

d)

⬜ + ⬜ = ⬜

4 How many altogether?

⬜ + ⬜ = ⬜

5 Draw a story picture for 5 + 5.

CHALLENGE

Reflect

Tell a partner a story for 4 + 1.

Date: _____

Find the missing number

1 Draw more to make 5.

How many did you add?

a)

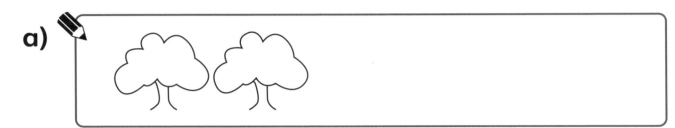

$2 + \boxed{} = 5$

b)

$4 + \boxed{} = 5$

2 Add more to make 6.

a)

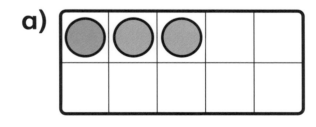

$3 + \boxed{} = 6$

b)

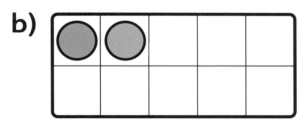

$2 + \boxed{} = 6$

3 Draw dots in the boxes to make the total.

a)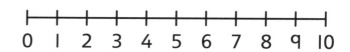

b)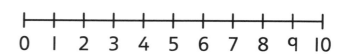

c)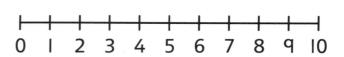

4 Write the missing parts.

a)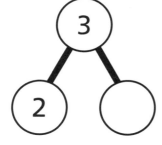

$2 + \boxed{} = 3$

b)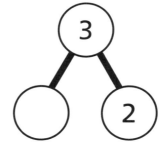

$\boxed{} + 2 = 3$

5 Write the missing parts.

$9 + \boxed{} = 10$ $\boxed{} + 1 = 9$

$8 + \boxed{} = 10$ $\boxed{} + 2 = 9$

$7 + \boxed{} = 10$ $\boxed{} + 3 = 9$

$6 + \boxed{} = 10$ $\boxed{} + 4 = 9$

What do you notice? Discuss with a partner.

Reflect

Tell a partner how to work out

$4 + \boxed{} = 7$

Make up your own missing number problem.

Give it to your partner to solve.

End of unit check

My journal

Circle an odd one out.

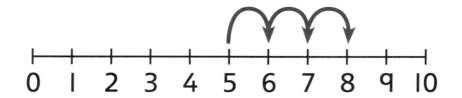

$10 = 5 + 5$

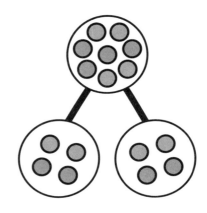

Discuss your odd one out with a partner.

These words will help you.

part   **whole**

total

add   **number**

Power check

How do you feel about your work in this unit?

Power play

A game for 2 players.

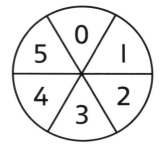

You will need:
- two different coloured counters.

1	2	3	4	5	6	7	8	9	10

How to play:

- Each player chooses two numbers from the circle.

- Each player adds their two numbers and puts a counter on a number track to show the total.

- Repeat.

- The counter must be placed on a different number each time.

86

How many are left? ❶

❶ How many are left?

→ Textbook 1A p120

a)

b)

c)
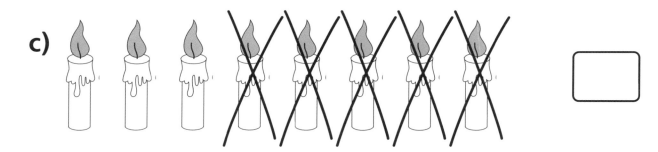

② Mo eats 3 apples.

How many apples are left?

3 **a)** There are 6 trees.

I tree is cut down.

How many trees are left?

b) There are 9 trees.

2 trees are cut down.

How many trees are left?

4 There are 10 birds.

☐ birds fly away.

☐ birds are left.

5 There are 7 toy cars.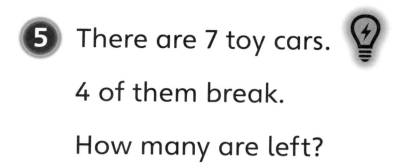

4 of them break.

How many are left?

6 2 balloons pop. There are 3 left.

CHALLENGE

How many balloons were there at the start?

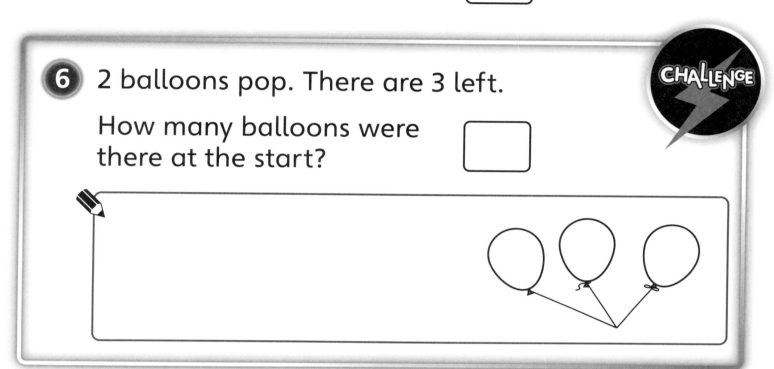

Reflect

How many are left?

What subtraction stories can you see here?

Tell a partner.

Date: _____

How many are left? ❷

1 There are 6 eggs.

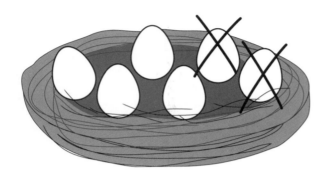

2 eggs break.

How many eggs are left?

6 − 2 = ☐

2 Complete the number sentences.

a)

8 − 3 = ☐

b)

6 − 5 = ☐

3 Complete the number sentences.

a)

4 − 2 = ☐

b)

8 − 4 = ☐

4 Complete the number sentences.

Use the ten frames to help you.

a) 10 − 5 = ☐

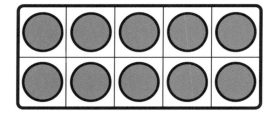

b) 10 − 7 = ☐

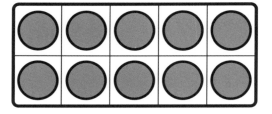

5 Complete each number sentence.

a)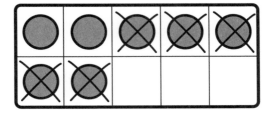

$7 - 5 =$ ☐

c)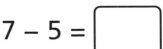

$4 - 1 =$ ☐

d)

$8 - 3 =$ ☐

b)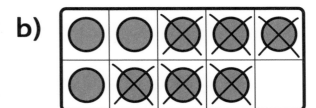

☐ $-$ ☐ $=$ ☐

e) $7 - 5 =$ ☐

f) $4 - 4 =$ ☐

Reflect

Show a partner why $5 - 2 = 3$.

I can show this with cubes.

Break apart ❶

1 There are 8 fish.

2 are .

The rest are .

Complete the part-whole model.

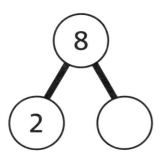

I will use a number bond or counters to help me.

2 Complete the part-whole model.

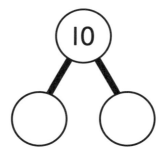

→ Textbook 1A p128

3 Complete the part-whole models.

a)

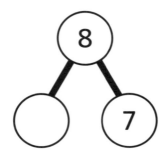

c)

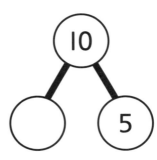

b)

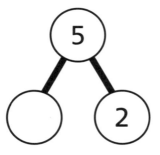

d)

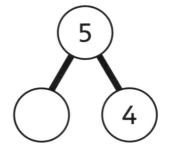

4 Write the missing numbers.

a) $2 + \boxed{} = 4$

e) $\boxed{} + 3 = 4$

b) $6 + \boxed{} = 7$

f) $\boxed{} + 2 = 8$

c) $3 + \boxed{} = 9$

g) $\boxed{} + 6 = 8$

d) $3 + \boxed{} = 10$

h) $\boxed{} + 3 = 3$

5 3 cubes belong to Tess.

How many cubes belong to Mia?

CHALLENGE

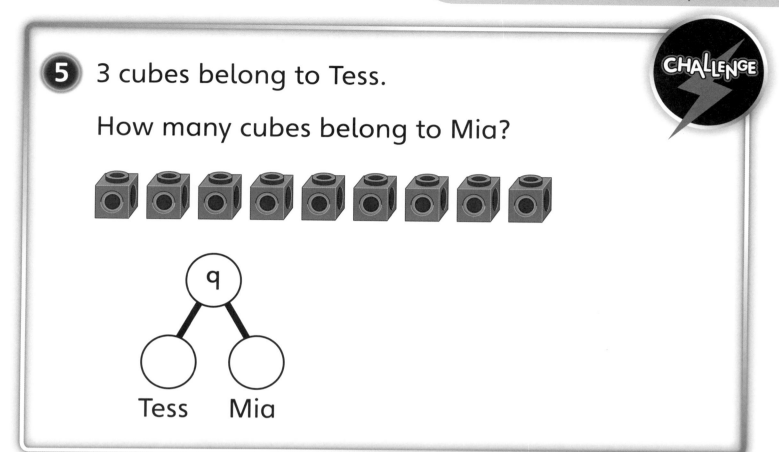

Tess   Mia

Reflect

$$8 - \boxed{} = 5$$

Tell a partner how they can work out the missing number.

Date: _____

Break apart ❷

1 Complete the subtractions.

a)

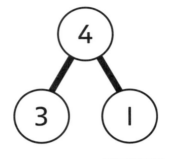

$4 - 3 = \boxed{}$

b)

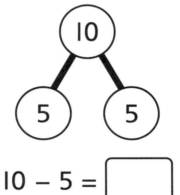

$10 - 5 = \boxed{}$

c)

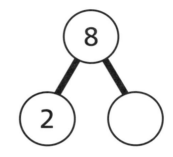

$8 - 2 = \boxed{}$

d)

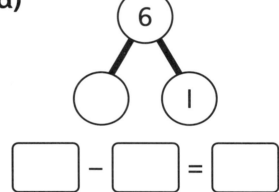

$\boxed{} - \boxed{} = \boxed{}$

2 There are 8 pieces of fruit in total.

5 are apples.

How many are **not** apples?

$8 - \boxed{} = \boxed{}$

a) There are 9 mice in total.

There are 4 big mice.

How many small mice are there?

b) There are 9 cats in total.

There are 6 big cats.

How many small cats are there?

 There are 9 cubes in total.

4 cubes are red, the rest are white.

How many cubes are white?

5 Complete the subtractions.

a) 7 – 6 = ☐

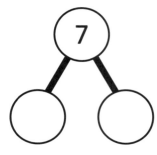

b) 9 – 2 = ☐

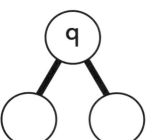

I will use my number bonds to help me.

Reflect

Discuss the two mistakes with a partner.

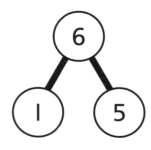

5 – 1 = 6

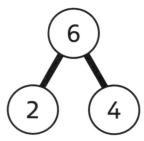

4 – 6 = 2

Fact families

1 Look at the frogs.

a) Complete the sentences.

There are ☐ frogs in total.

☐ are on lily pads.

☐ are swimming.

b) Complete the part-whole model.

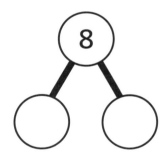

c) Complete the fact family.

☐ + ☐ = 8   8 − ☐ = ☐

☐ + ☐ = 8   8 − ☐ = ☐

2 Complete the fact family.

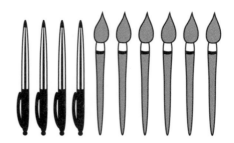

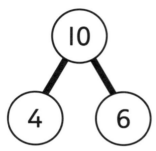

☐ + ☐ = ☐

☐ + ☐ = ☐

☐ − ☐ = ☐

☐ − ☐ = ☐

3 Complete the part-whole model and fact family for the picture.

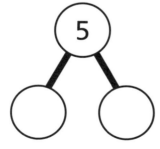

☐ + ☐ = ☐

☐ + ☐ = ☐

☐ − ☐ = ☐

☐ − ☐ = ☐

④ Use the part-whole model to complete the fact family.

CHALLENGE

⬜ + ⬜ = ⬜

⬜ + ⬜ = ⬜

⬜ − ⬜ = ⬜

⬜ − ⬜ = ⬜

10
3 7

⬜ = ⬜ ◯ ⬜

⬜ = ⬜ ◯ ⬜

⬜ = ⬜ ◯ ⬜

⬜ = ⬜ ◯ ⬜

Reflect

I know 2 + 4 = 6.

Discuss with a partner what else you know.

Date: _____

Subtraction on a number line

1 **a)** The 🦘 makes 6 jumps back from 10.

Where does it land?

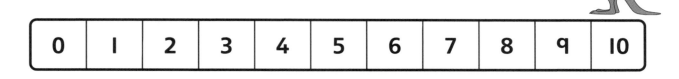

| 0 | 1 | 2 | 3 | 4 | 5 | 6 | 7 | 8 | 9 | 10 |

b) The 🦘 makes 4 jumps back from 7.

Where does it land?

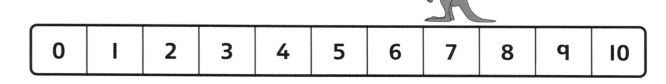

| 0 | 1 | 2 | 3 | 4 | 5 | 6 | 7 | 8 | 9 | 10 |

2 How many jumps does the frog make to catch the fly?

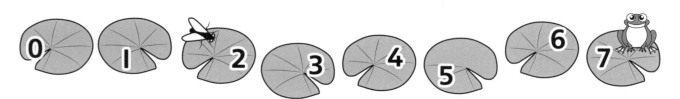

7 – ☐ = 2

3 Use the number lines to complete the subtractions.

a) 9 – 2 = ☐

0 1 2 3 4 5 6 7 8 9 10

b) 10 – 6 = ☐

0 1 2 3 4 5 6 7 8 9 10

c) ☐ = 10 – 4

0 1 2 3 4 5 6 7 8 9 10

4 Complete the subtractions.

a) 8 – 3 = ☐

0 1 2 3 4 5 6 7 8 9 10

b) 8 – ☐ = 7

0 1 2 3 4 5 6 7 8 9 10

c) ☐ – 6 = 0

0 1 2 3 4 5 6 7 8 9 10

CHALLENGE

5 Write five different subtractions.

They should all have the answer 5.

The first one has been done for you.

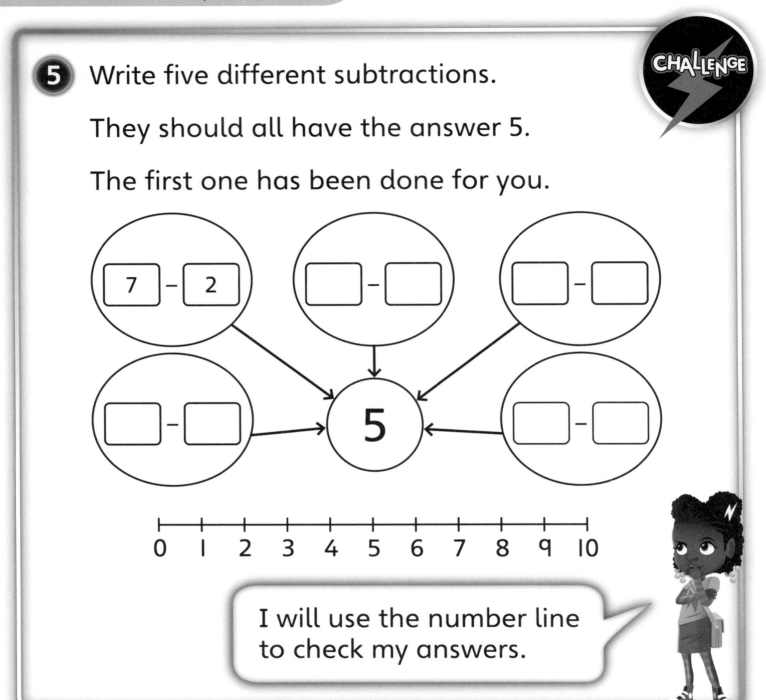

I will use the number line to check my answers.

Reflect

There are lots of ways to subtract.

Discuss what you could do with a partner.

Add or subtract 1 or 2

1 Work out

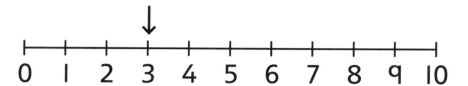

$3 + 1 = \boxed{}$ $3 + 2 = \boxed{}$

2 Work out

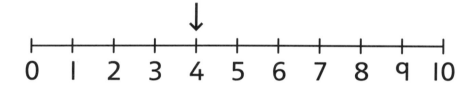

$4 - 1 = \boxed{}$ $4 - 2 = \boxed{}$

3 Work out

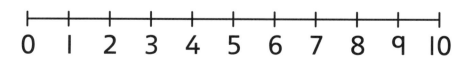

a) $2 + 2 = \boxed{}$ c) $3 - 2 = \boxed{}$

b) $4 + 2 = \boxed{}$ d) $5 - 2 = \boxed{}$

4

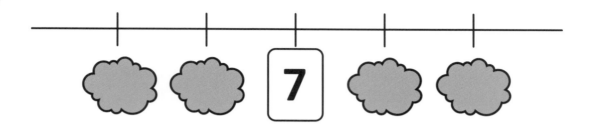

a) $7 + 1 =$ ▢

b) $7 + 2 =$ ▢

c) $7 - 1 =$ ▢

d) $7 - 2 =$ ▢

5 Solve these additions and subtractions.

a) $5 + 1 =$ ▢

b) $6 + 2 =$ ▢

c) $8 + 1 =$ ▢

d) $2 + 1 =$ ▢

e) $5 + 2 =$ ▢

f) $9 + 1 =$ ▢

g) $5 - 1 =$ ▢

h) $6 - 2 =$ ▢

i) $8 - 1 =$ ▢

j) $2 - 1 =$ ▢

k) $5 - 2 =$ ▢

l) $9 - 1 =$ ▢

CHALLENGE

6 Join the matching pairs.

3 + 1	8 + 2
6 + 1	4 + 2
5 + 1	5 + 2
8 + 1	7 + 2
9 + 1	2 + 2

Reflect

Solve each addition and subtraction.

$4 + 1 = \boxed{}$ $\qquad$ $4 - 1 = \boxed{}$

$4 + 2 = \boxed{}$ $\qquad$ $4 - 2 = \boxed{}$

Tell a partner what you notice.

Date: _____

Solve word problems – addition and subtraction

1 Zac has 8 sweets.

He gives 3 to Kara.

How many sweets does Zac have left?

8 – ☐ = ☐

Zac has ☐ sweets.

2 Amy has 3 cubes.

She gets 5 more.

How many cubes does Amy have now?

3 + ☐ = ☐

Amy has ☐ cubes.

3 Lucy has **6** apples.

She eats **2** apples.

How many apples are left?

☐ – ☐ = ☐

There are ☐ apples left.

4 Complete the number sentences.

Match them to the cubes.

3 + 2 = ☐

8 – 3 = ☐

5 + 3 = ☐

7 – 3 = ☐

5 Look at this shape puzzle.

▨ + ▨ = 10

▨ + ▲ = 8

▲ − ⬤ = 1

What number does each shape stand for?

▨ = ☐   ▲ = ☐   ⬤ = ☐

Reflect

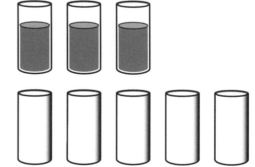

Use the picture to write your own maths question.

_____

_____

_____

End of unit check

My journal

Izzy says she can see two facts.

$6 = 3 + 3$ $3 + 3 = 6$

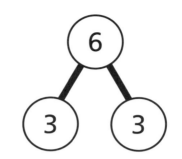

Fred says he can see three facts.

$6 - 3 = 3$ $3 - 6 = 3$ $3 = 6 - 3$

Explain the mistake that Fred has made.

The mistake is _____

because _____

_____ .

These words will help you.

part   whole   add

subtract   equals

take away

Power check

How do you feel about your work in this unit?

Power puzzle

| 0 | 1 | 2 | 3 | 4 | 5 |

Choose cards to complete the sentence.

$\square - \square = 1$

$\square + \square = 5$

We all need practice to get this right!

How many different answers can you find?

2 +   Good try

4 +   Good work

6 +   Awesome work

Recognise and name 3D shapes

→ Textbook 1A p156

1 **a)** Circle the cubes.

b) Circle the pyramids.

2 Circle the odd one out.

a)

b)

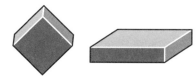 

c)

  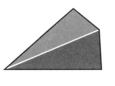

3 Look at the picture.

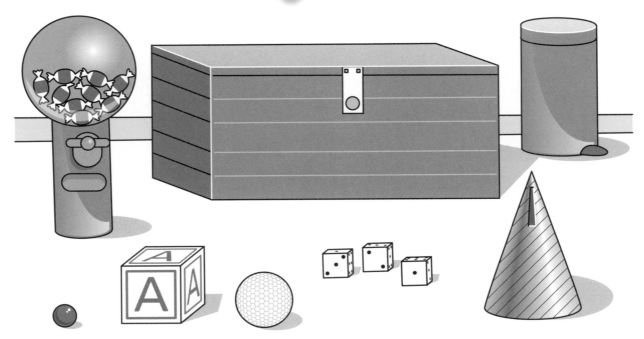

a) How many cubes are there?

There are ☐ cubes.

b) How many spheres are there?

There are ☐ spheres.

c) How many cylinders are there?

There are ☐ cylinders.

4 Name the hidden shapes.

CHALLENGE

| sphere | pyramid | cube | cuboid |

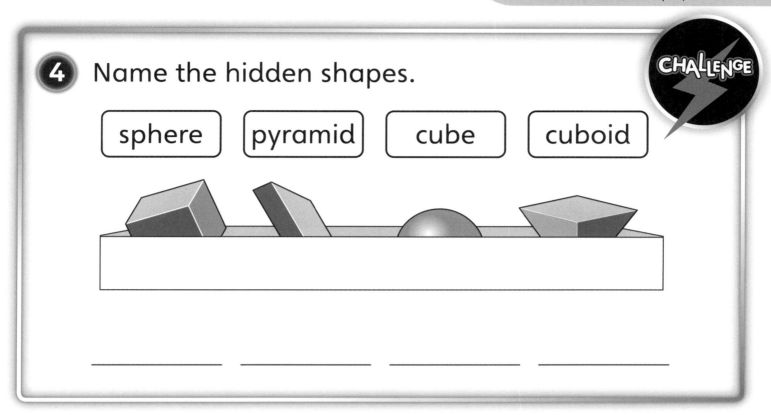

_____ _____ _____ _____

Reflect

Where can you find different shapes at school or at home?

Where can you find a pyramid?

 _____
 _____
_____

Date: _____

Sort 3D shapes

1 Match each shape to its name.

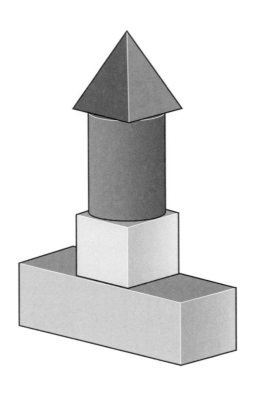

cube

cylinder

pyramid

cuboid

2 Circle the cuboids.

3 Tick the sentences that are true.

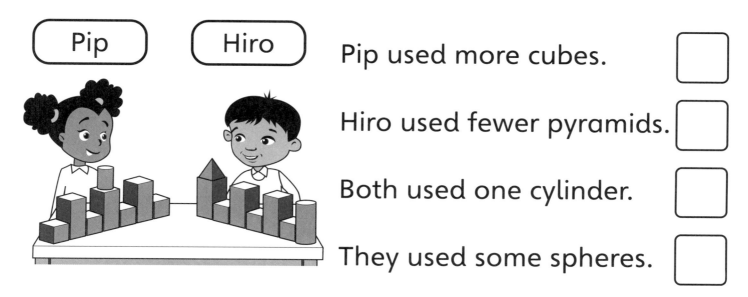

Pip   Hiro

Pip used more cubes. ☐

Hiro used fewer pyramids. ☐

Both used one cylinder. ☐

They used some spheres. ☐

4 Match the boxes to the objects.

2 spheres
I cone
I cuboid

I cuboid
I pyramid
2 cylinders

I cube
I cuboid
I cylinder
I sphere

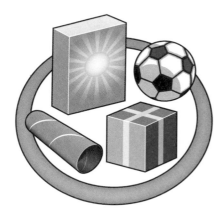

5 Write the correct letters in each hoop.

CHALLENGE

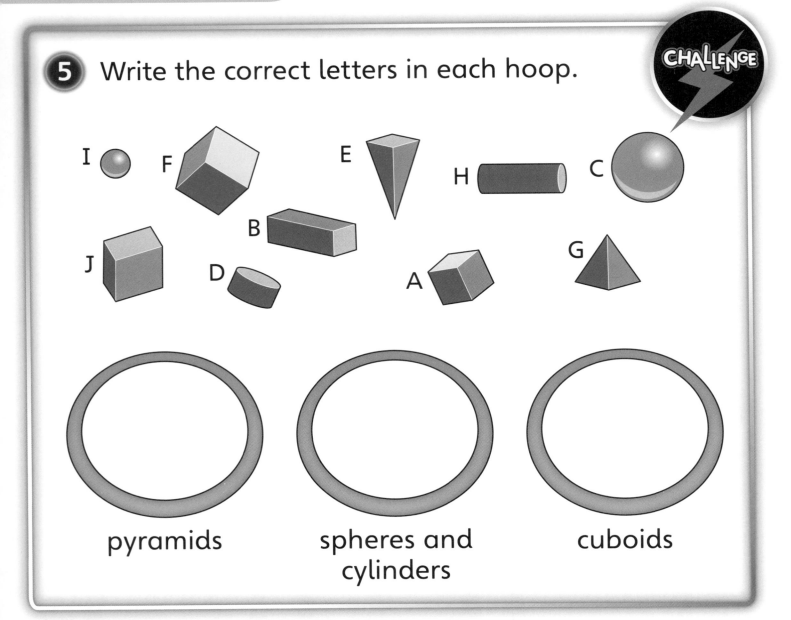

pyramids

spheres and cylinders

cuboids

Reflect

Name 5 different 3D shapes.

_____, _____, _____,

_____, _____ .

I will look for each shape in the classroom.

Date: _____

Recognise and name 2D shapes

1 Match each shape to the correct name.

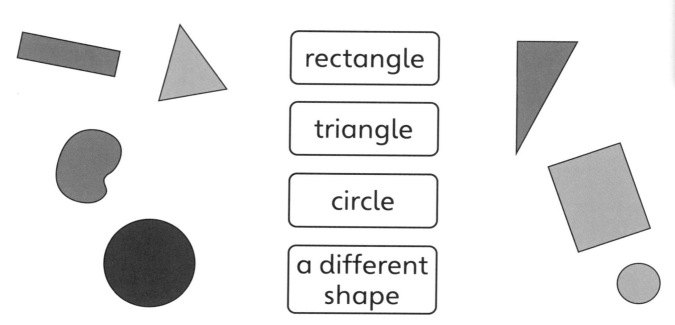

rectangle

triangle

circle

a different shape

2 Circle the odd one out.

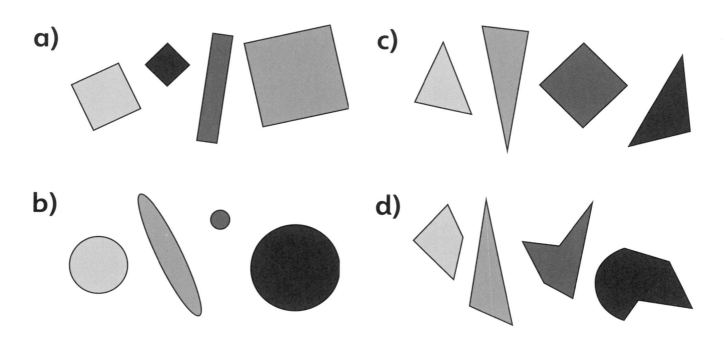

a)

c)

b)

d)

Textbook 1A p164

3 Name the shapes.

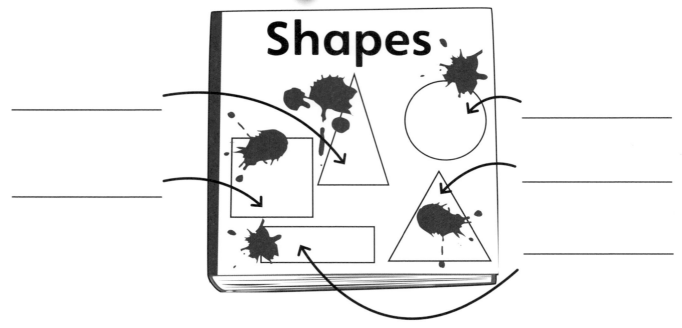

_____

_____

_____

_____

_____

4 Draw a rectangle using 6 squares.

5 Colour and count the shapes.

CHALLENGE

Colours used:

☐ = circles

☐ = rectangles

☐ = triangles

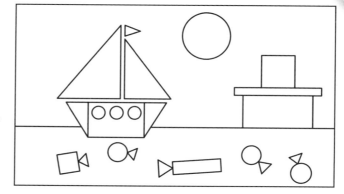

a) There are ☐ circles.

b) There are ☐ rectangles.

c) There are ☐ triangles.

Reflect

Name the different shapes.

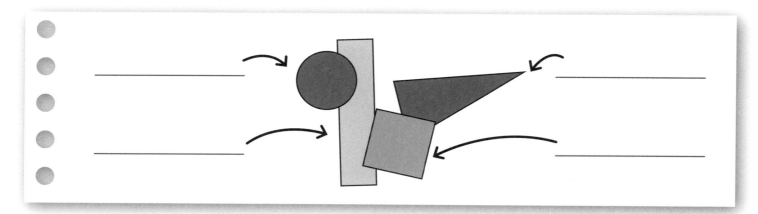

_____   _____

_____   _____

Date: _____

Sort 2D shapes

1 Join the 3D shapes to the 2D shapes they print.

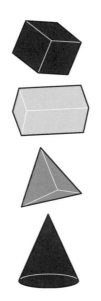

2 Cross out the 2D shapes that the 3D shape cannot print.

a)

b)

3 Complete each sentence.

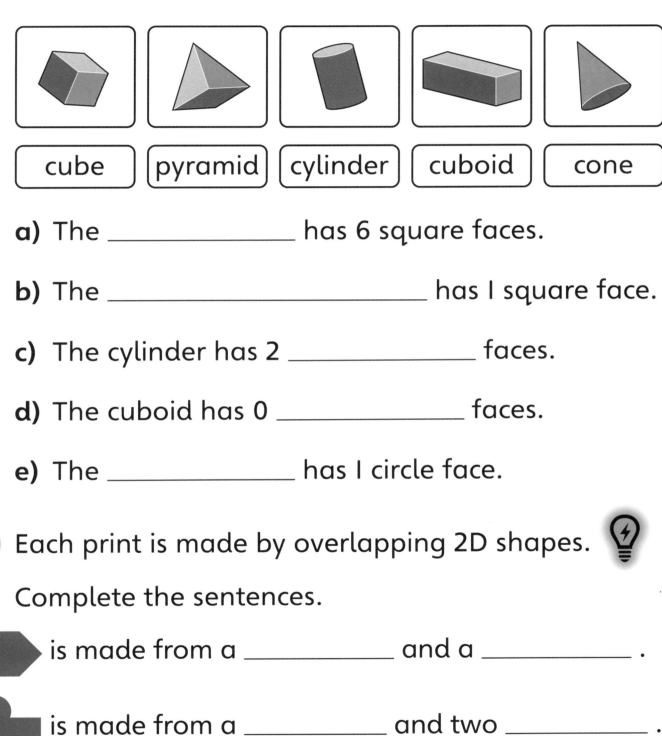

cube | pyramid | cylinder | cuboid | cone

a) The _____ has 6 square faces.

b) The _____ has 1 square face.

c) The cylinder has 2 _____ faces.

d) The cuboid has 0 _____ faces.

e) The _____ has 1 circle face.

4 Each print is made by overlapping 2D shapes.

Complete the sentences.

is made from a _____ and a _____ .

is made from a _____ and two _____ .

is made from a _____ and a _____ .

123

5 Match the shapes with the order they were printed.

CHALLENGE

rectangle

square

triangle

circle

first

second

third

fourth

fifth

sixth

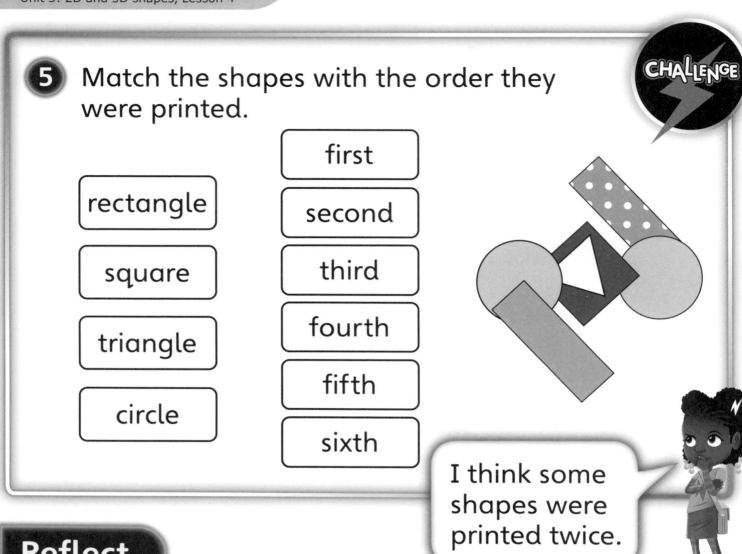

I think some shapes were printed twice.

Reflect

Match the name and the shape.

square   cuboid   triangle

cube   rectangle   pyramid

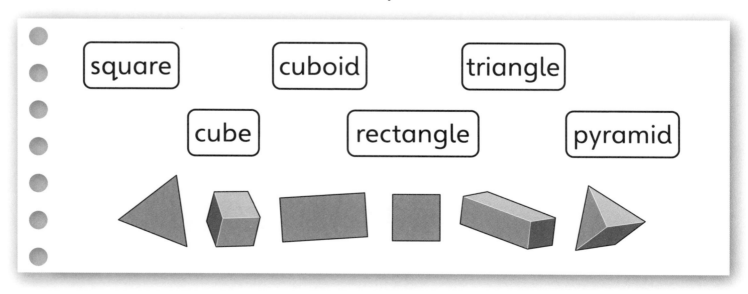

Make patterns with shapes

1 Continue the pattern.

a)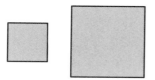

b)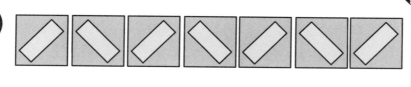

2 Tick the shapes missing from the patterns.

a)

A    B 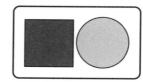   C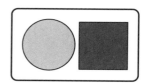

b)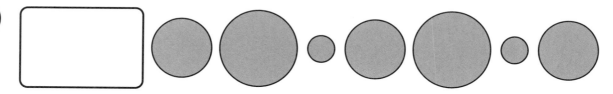

A 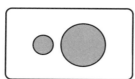   B 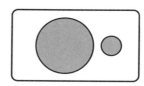   C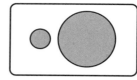

3 Circle each repeating part.

Complete the sentences.

a)
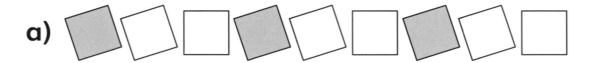

The pattern has ☐ repeating shapes.

b)

The pattern has ☐ repeating shapes.

4 Tick the shape that continues each pattern.

a)
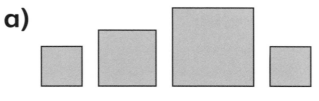

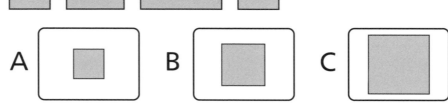

A   B   C

b)
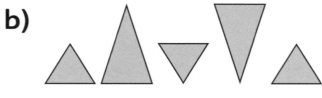

A   B   C   D

5 Complete the part-whole models to
continue the pattern.

CHALLENGE

a)

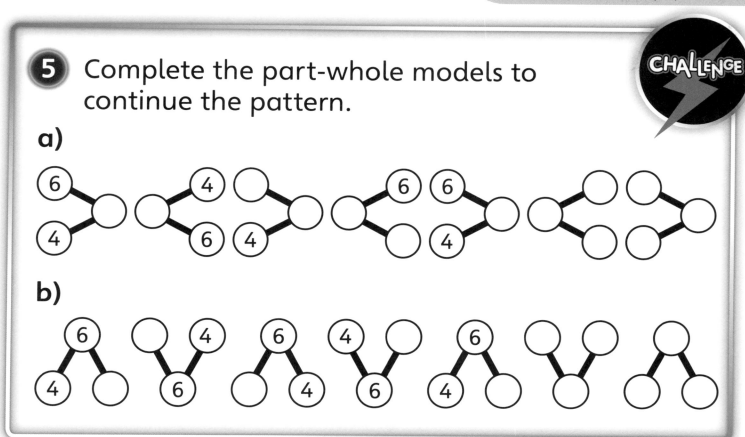

b)

Reflect

Make a repeating pattern with any of these shapes.

Hide some of the shapes.

Ask a partner to work out the pattern.

Date: _____

End of unit check

My journal

→ Textbook 1A p176

Draw this shape in the correct group.

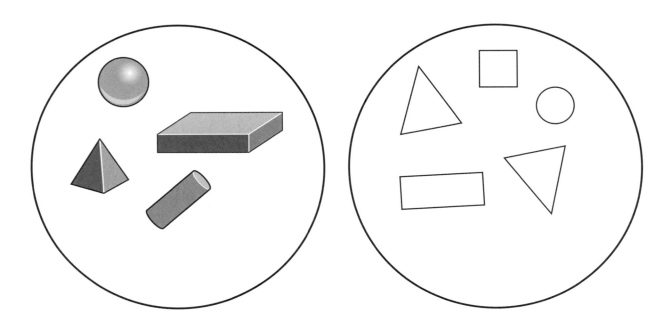

Discuss your choices with a partner.

These words
will help you.

dark   **light**

shape

2D   **3D**   **group**

Power check

How do you feel about your work in this unit?

Power puzzle

Choose three colours.

Colour the shapes so that shapes of the same colour only touch at a corner.

Find four different ways.

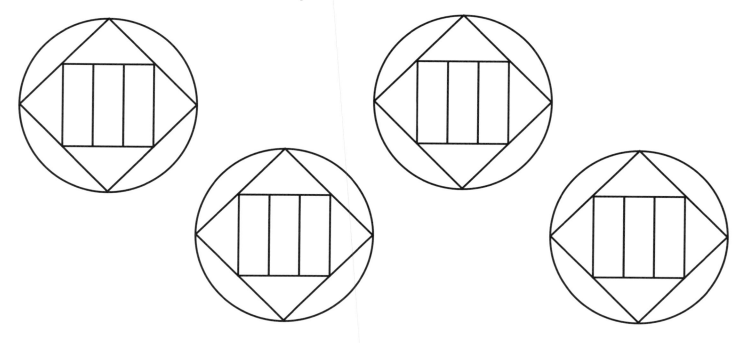

My Power Points

Colour in the ☆ to show what you have learnt.

Colour in the ☺ if you feel happy about what you have learnt.

Unit 1
I can …

☆ ☺ Sort and count objects to 10

☆ ☺ Represent numbers to 10

☆ ☺ Count one more and one less

☆ ☺ Count backwards from 10 to 0

☆ ☺ Compare and order numbers

☆ ☺ Use a number line

Unit 2
I can …

☆ ☺ Use a part-whole model

☆ ☺ Write number sentences

☆ ☺ Find different ways to make a number

☆ ☺ Make number bonds up to 10

Unit 3

I can …

☆ ☺ Add parts to find the whole

☆ ☺ Add more

☆ ☺ Find a missing part

☆ ☺ Solve word problems

Unit 4

I can …

☆ ☺ Take away to find how many are left

☆ ☺ Break the whole into parts

☆ ☺ Discover related number facts

☆ ☺ Solve word problems

Unit 5

I can …

☆ ☺ Name and sort 3D shapes

☆ ☺ Name and sort 2D shapes

☆ ☺ Make patterns with shapes

Wow! Look how much you can do!

You can use these for your working out.

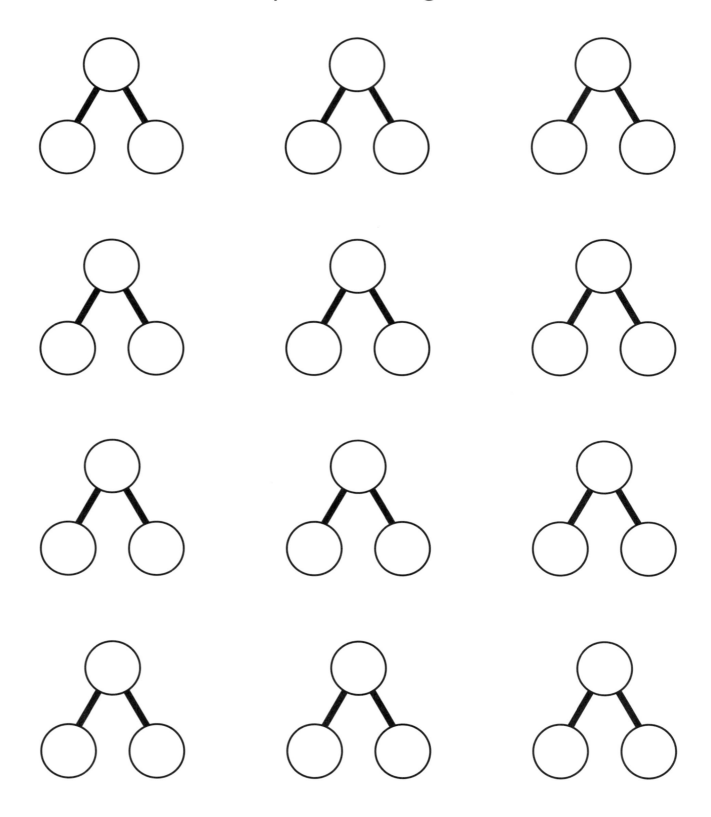

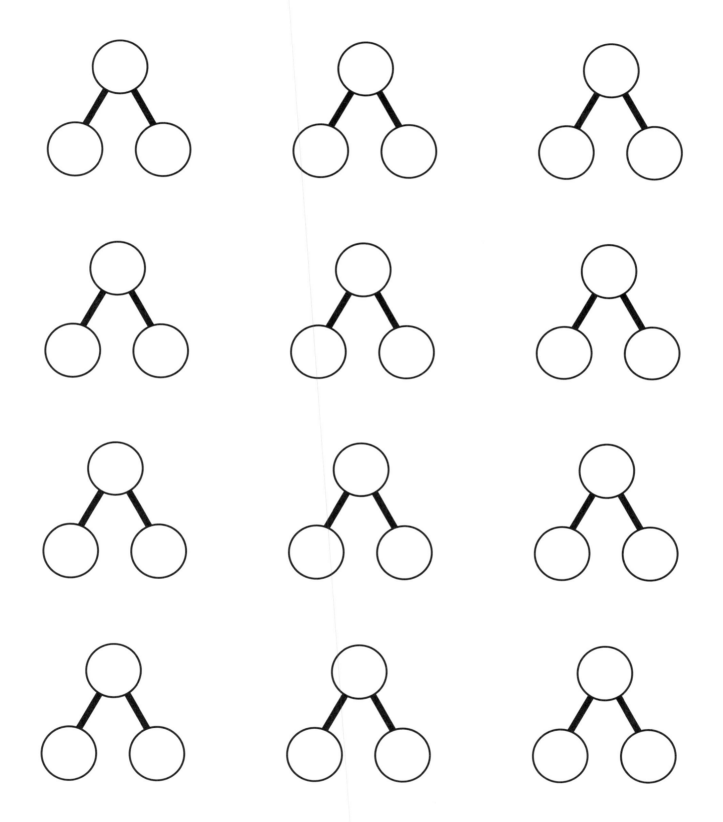

You can use these for your working out.

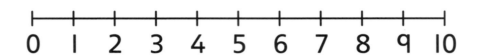

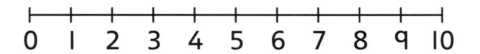

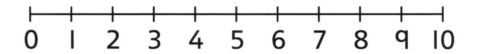

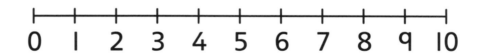

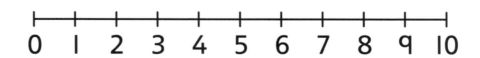

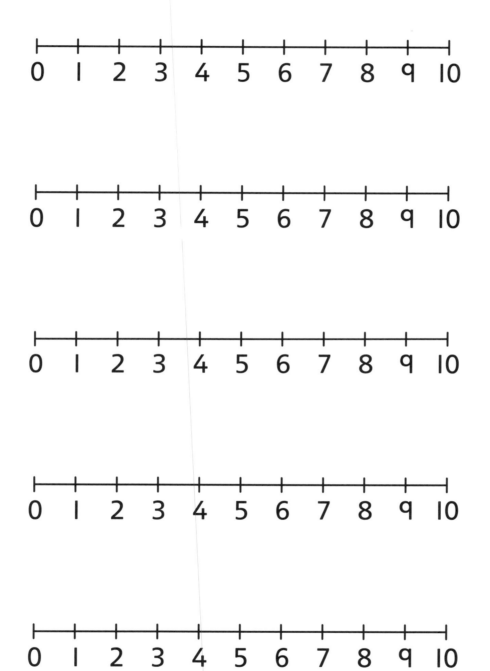

Published by Pearson Education Limited, 80 Strand, London, WC2R 0RL.

www.pearsonschools.co.uk

Text © Pearson Education Limited 2017, 2022
Edited by Pearson and Florence Production Ltd
First edition edited by Pearson, Little Grey Cells Publishing Services and Haremi Ltd
Designed and typeset by Pearson and Florence Production Ltd
First edition designed and typeset by Kamae Design
Original illustrations © Pearson Education Limited 2017, 2022
Illustrated by Laura Arias, John Batten, Paul Moran and Nadene Naude at Beehive Illustration;
and Florence Production Ltd and Kamae Design
Cover design by Pearson Education Ltd
Front and back cover illustrations by Will Overton at Advocate Art and Nadene Naude at Beehive
Illustration
Series editor: Tony Staneff; Lead author: Josh Lury
Authors (first edition): Tony Staneff, Josh Lury, Beth Smith, Dan Zhang and Lihua Luang
Consultants (first edition): Professor Liu Jian and Professor Zhang Dan

The rights of Tony Staneff and Josh Lury to be identified as authors of this work have been
asserted by them in accordance with the Copyright, Designs and Patents Act 1988.

First published 2017
This edition first published 2022

26 25 24 23
10 9 8 7 6 5 4 3 2

British Library Cataloguing in Publication Data
A catalogue record for this book is available from the British Library

ISBN 978 1 292 41936 7

Printed in the UK by Bell & Bain Ltd, Glasgow

For Power Maths online resources, go to:
www.activelearnprimary.co.uk

Note from the publisher
Pearson has robust editorial processes, including answer and fact checks, to ensure the accuracy of
the content in this publication, and every effort is made to ensure this publication is free of errors.
We are, however, only human, and occasionally errors do occur. Pearson is not liable for any
misunderstandings that arise as a result of errors in this publication, but it is our priority to ensure
that the content is accurate. If you spot an error, please do contact us at resourcescorrections@
pearson.com so we can make sure it is corrected.